EDGE
BOOKS ™

Wild Stunts

AMAZING
ANIMAL
STUNTS

Edge Books are published by Capstone Press,
1710 Roe Crest Drive, North Mankato, Minnesota 56003
www.capstonepub.com

Library of Congress Cataloging-in-Publication Data
Simons, Lisa M. B., 1969– author.
 Amazing animal stunts / by Lisa M. Bolt Simons.
    pages cm. — (Edge books. Wild stunts)
 Summary: "Describes animal stunts, including who accomplished these stunts and, to a certain
degree, how" — Provided by publisher.
 Audience: Ages 8-9
 Audience: Grades 4 to 6
 Includes bibliographical references and index.
 ISBN 978-1-4914-4253-1 (library binding)
 ISBN 978-1-4914-4314-9 (eBook PDF)
1. Animal training — Juvenile literature. 2. Animal behavior — Juvenile literature. I. Title.
 GV1829.S56 2016
 636.088'8 — dc23   2015002859

Editorial Credits
Nate LeBoutillier, editor; Kyle Grenz, designer; Jo Miller, media researcher; Tori Abraham,
production specialist

Photo Credits
AP Images: The Bulletin/Lyle Cox, 27, The Repository/Scott Heckel, 17; Gamma-Keystone via
Getty Images/Keystone-France, 11; Gentleshaw Wildlife Centre/Katie Smith, 18-19; Landov:
Reuters/K9 Storm Inc, 10; Newscom: EPA/Paul Hilton, 6-7, EPA/Rungroj Yongrit, 23, Pacific
Photos/Dan Callister, 8, Photoshot, 12, Reuters/Jim Bourg, 24, Reuters/Joshua Lott, 20, Sipa
USA/Alex Milan Tracy, cover, 14, 15, Splash News/Solent News, 21, ZUMA Press/Scott Mc
Kiernan, 28-29, ZUMA Press/St Petersburg Times, 4-5; Newspix via Getty Images/Tim Marsden,
25; Wikimedia, 16

Design Elements
Shutterstock: antishock, Igorsky, Leigh Prather, Moriz, Radoman Durkovic

Direct Quotations
Page 7: September 14, 2014, e-mail response to author; interview interpreted and transcribed by
Yuri Hosono
Page 9: September 15, 2014, e-mail response to author
Page 19: September 15, 2014, phone interview with author
page 26: December 9, 2014, e-mail response to author
page 29: July 20, 2001, The New York Times, "Gunther Gebel-Williams, Circus Animal Trainer,
Dies at 66" by Richard Severo, http://www.nytimes.com/2001/07/20/arts/gunther-gebel-
williams-circus-animal-trainer-dies-at-66.html

Printed in the United States of America in North Mankato, Minnesota.
032015   008823CGF15

Table of Contents

Awesome Animals
and Their Jaw-Dropping Acts. 4

Dynamite Dogs. 6

Other Four-Legged Creatures 14

Feathered and
Finned Friends 18

Tame Tricks
by Wild Animals. 22

Glossary. 30
Read More. 31
Internet Sites 31
Index. 32

Awesome Animals and Their Jaw-Dropping Acts

What makes people enjoy amazing animal stunts? Is it because animals seem out of place trying such tricks? Does it astonish people that animals can do some of the same things as humans? Maybe it's that animal stunts seem amusing, unbelievable, and bizarre all at the same time. Whatever the reason, we must remember that most animals are capable of more than we imagine. Animal stunts and tricks take time, patience, and hard work.

Most animals respond to training. You've likely seen dogs that sit, fetch, or roll over on command. But have you ever seen a dog that could skip rope, fly, or read? Or a cat that could play a musical instrument? Sometimes an amazing stunt makes the average pet look not-so-average.

Wild animals stunts can be just as impressive. Like when an owl rides a bike. Or elephants create art. Or a monkey uses *technology*. Animals and their tricks may make your jaw drop in amazement.

technology—the use of science to do practical things, such as designing complex machines

Dynamite Dogs

Hopping Hounds

Meet 13 dogs owned by the Uchida Show Business Company in Fujiyoshida, Japan. They not only skip rope. They skip rope at the same time. Yoshihiro Uchida is the second-generation owner of the company. He says that all his employees train the dogs. This way, the dogs learn to trust all the trainers. If one trainer quits, the dogs still work with people they know. Currently, his company employs five trainers.

Uchida's family started a dog circus in the 1950s in order to have jobs while protecting stray dogs. They've always wanted to help people learn not to abandon dogs.

"Jumping rope is the best way for dogs to enjoy training without using a lot of tools."
Yoshihiro Uchida

After a 30-minute practice, the dogs rest for an hour. This process is repeated a few times a day. Some dogs like treats during training. Other dogs prefer praise. For some dogs, it takes three months to master skipping rope alone. For other dogs, it can take up to 10 months. Then the dogs need to train two or three months more to perform together.

CHECK THIS OUT!

Geronimo, a cattle dog mix, can **double dutch**. Owner Samantha Valle trained her several hours a day for five weeks. One part of the stunt includes Geronimo jumping on a stick in the middle of the ropes. This is so she'll stay in place. Geronimo's jumping record is 128 times a minute!

double dutch—a jump-rope game with two long jump ropes swung in opposite directions so that they cross rhythmically

7

The Fabulous Willow

A spitz/terrier cross named Willow became better at reading and math than most toddlers and kindergartners. To teach Willow to read, Willow's owner Lyssa Howells chose six words. The words were "wave," "bang," "sit up," "sit," and "Nutrish," a dog food brand.

Howells started with voice commands. Then Howells used flashcards with her voice. Finally, Howells just used the cards. Willow would do what the card said. The whole training process took just six weeks. Howells used food as a reward.

Lyssa Howells and her reading dog, Willow

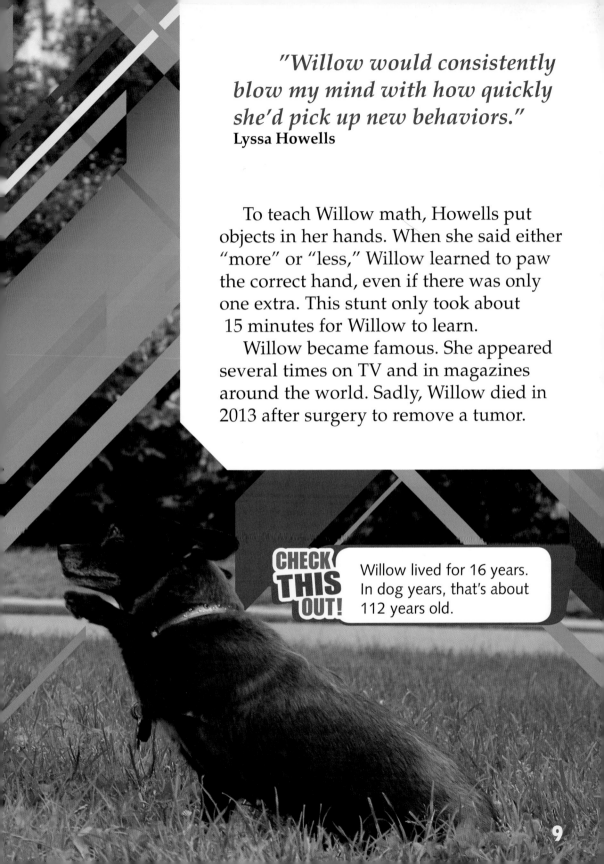

"Willow would consistently blow my mind with how quickly she'd pick up new behaviors."
Lyssa Howells

To teach Willow math, Howells put objects in her hands. When she said either "more" or "less," Willow learned to paw the correct hand, even if there was only one extra. This stunt only took about 15 minutes for Willow to learn.

Willow became famous. She appeared several times on TV and in magazines around the world. Sadly, Willow died in 2013 after surgery to remove a tumor.

CHECK THIS OUT!

Willow lived for 16 years. In dog years, that's about 112 years old.

Mike Forsyth and Cara in mid-air action

Four-Legged Flyers

Did you know dogs can fly? Cara is a Beauceron search and rescue dog. Cara's owner is Mike Forsythe, a canine parachute instructor. Together, Cara and Forsythe completed the highest canine HALO *parachute* jump to date. HALO stands for "high altitude, low opening." It is a term often used in the military. How high were the pair? About as high as an airplane flies: 30,100 feet (9,175 m)! Both Cara and Forsythe wore oxygen masks.

parachute—a large piece of strong, lightweight fabric; parachutes allow people to jump from high places and float slowly and safely to the ground

winged suit—a garment that allows a person to glide through the air when in free fall, with sections of fabric between the arms and legs that inflate when the wearer jumps from an aircraft or high place

A dog named Whisper is another high flyer. She rides with owner Dean Potter when he BASE jumps. BASE stands for "building, antenna, space, and Earth." Potter wears a **winged suit**, jumps off big mountains, and soars through the air. Whisper rides in a special backpack that has a hole for her head. A parachute helps them land on the ground safely. Potter first carried Whisper on hikes to get her used to heights. Now Whisper heads for her pack whenever Potter puts on his wing suit.

CHECK THIS OUT!

Dogs have been part of military efforts throughout history. In World War II, the 13th Parachute Battalion of the British Army employed parachuting dogs.

A Mutt That Marvels

Omar von Muller is a Hollywood trainer who works with talented *canines*. Uggie is a Jack Russell terrier who once had problems behaving. No one wanted Uggie, and he was on his way to the pound. Von Muller saved Uggie and trained him so well that Uggie appeared in the movies. In the 2011 film *The Artist,* Uggie won moviegoers' hearts by acting out a number of tricks. He played dead, walked on his hind legs, and covered his head to appear shy. His lively "expressions" seemed to rival the human actors' best work.

Uggie next to the book he "wrote"

Jumpy, a Border Collie mix, is another of von Muller's dogs. Jumpy can wink. He can walk on his two back legs. He can weave around orange cones by walking upside-down while doing a "paw" stand. Jumpy can do high back flips to catch a Frisbee. This amazing dog can also ride behind a boat on a **kneeboard**. He can ride a three-wheel scooter. Jumpy is also an ace on a skateboard.

CHECK THIS OUT!

Jumpy holds the record for the fastest 100 meters on a skateboard by a dog: 19.65 seconds. Uggie also rides a skateboard, though not as fast. He "wrote" a book in 2012 entitled *Uggie: My Story*.

canine—of or relating to dogs

kneeboard—a short board for surfing or waterskiing in a kneeling position

Other Four-Legged Creatures

Phenomenal Felines

Cats can't read music, but some can play it. Owner Samantha Martin, a former zookeeper, taught cats to "play" musical instruments. This *feline* band is called The Rock Cats. Though they play off-key, The Rock Cats are believed to be the only cat band in the world. They are part of a circus called The Amazing Acro-Cats. Martin's cats jump through hoops, roll on top of balls, walk high wires, and perform other amazing *feats*.

feline—to do with cats

feat—an achievement that shows great courage, strength, or skill

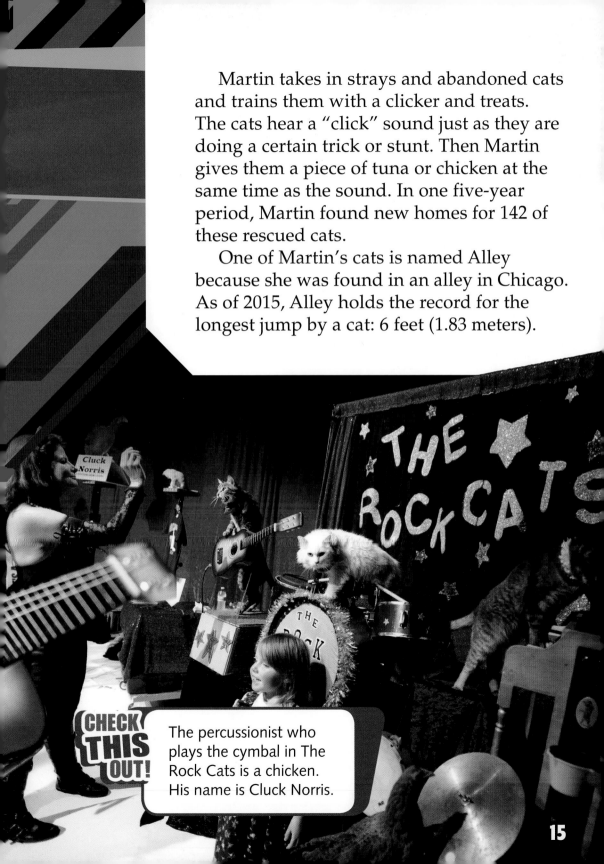

Martin takes in strays and abandoned cats and trains them with a clicker and treats. The cats hear a "click" sound just as they are doing a certain trick or stunt. Then Martin gives them a piece of tuna or chicken at the same time as the sound. In one five-year period, Martin found new homes for 142 of these rescued cats.

One of Martin's cats is named Alley because she was found in an alley in Chicago. As of 2015, Alley holds the record for the longest jump by a cat: 6 feet (1.83 meters).

CHECK THIS OUT!

The percussionist who plays the cymbal in The Rock Cats is a chicken. His name is Cluck Norris.

Captain Alberto Larraguibel
Morales jumping with Huaso

Leaps Great and Small

In 1933 a Thoroughbred horse originally named Faithful was born in Chile. Faithful was bred to race but was too twitchy and unruly. Faithful then trained to parade with the military but was injured and nearly died. The military switched Faithful to **stadium jumping**. It went poorly until one day, jumping without a rider on his back, Faithful went over a wall as tall as a man.

stadium jumping—a competition where horses and riders follow a course of hurdles or jumps within an arena or riding ring

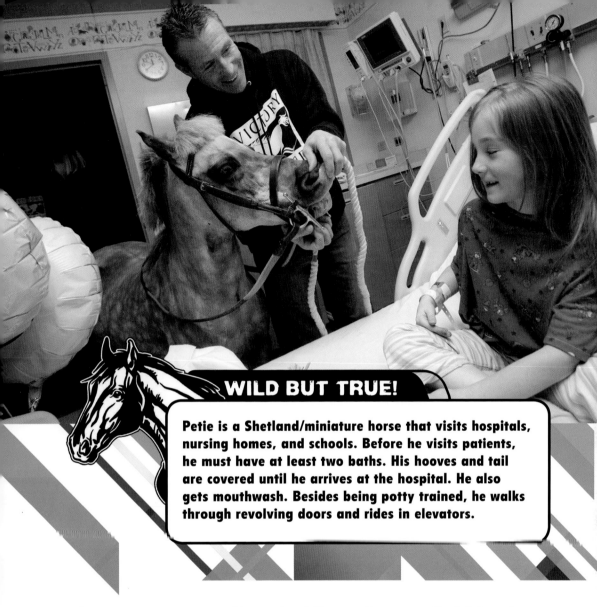

Captain Alberto Larraguibel Morales saw the horse jump. He bought Faithful and renamed him Huaso [How-so]. In 1949 the captain rode Huaso when he jumped 8 feet, 1.25 inches (2.47 m) over wooden poles. Though it happened more than 65 years ago, no horse has jumped as high since.

Feathered and Finned Friends

Treacle is not a normal tawny owl. Born in captivity, Treacle is now a tame and trained bird. For fun, Treacle rides on the handlebars of Jenny Morgan's bike. Morgan is Treacle's owner and the director of Gentleshaw Wildlife Centre in Staffordshire, United Kingdom.

Treacle learned to ride along on Morgan's bike when Morgan decided to get in shape. Morgan liked spending time with Treacle, so one day she placed the owl on her bike's handlebars. Treacle stayed put for a 30-minute ride. Sometimes, Morgan takes 16-year-old Treacle to the local woods. For exercise, Treacle flies. Then Morgan gets her exercise biking them back to the *sanctuary*.

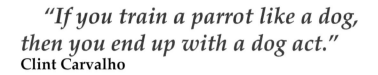

> *"If you train a parrot like a dog, then you end up with a dog act."*
> **Clint Carvalho**

Clint Carvalho, an exotic bird trainer, rescues abandoned or abused birds. He wanted Kitten, his white cockatoo, to find him about 600 feet (185 meters) away. He had no idea if the stunt would work because they hadn't trained for it. Carvalho stood on a theater stage for a filming of the TV show *America's Got Talent.* Kitten sat on a roof 160 feet (49 m) high across the street. Instead of flying away, she flew straight to her owner! Carvalho considers this the greatest bird stunt he has seen so far.

CHECK THIS OUT! Bird beaks have special adaptations for the food they eat. According to Carvalho, beaks act more like a hand than a weapon.

sanctuary—a natural area where birds or animals are protected from hunters

Why Fly When You Can Run?

At the annual Ostrich Festival in Chandler, Arizona, riders climb on ostriches' backs and hang on. The ostriches race at full speed, up to 43 miles (69.2 kilometers) per hour.

Animal trainer Steve Boger brings the ostriches to Chandler. He trained the birds about 30 minutes a day. It took less than a week. He didn't use food or rewards. He just used "home base," the place where the birds ate and slept. He also trained the ostriches to pull people in *chariots*.

CHECK THIS OUT! Tic-tac-toe chickens actually play the game against human opponents. Trained by Steve Boger's brother, Bunky, and his family, the hens rarely lose.

chariot—a light, two-wheeled cart pulled by horses

Comet the goldfish
shoots for two.

Fish With a Swish

A goldfish in Pennsylvania named Comet doesn't
perform just one stunt. Not even two stunts. Comet
can do several things. Comet limbos and fetches a
ring. He also plays football, soccer, and basketball.

His trainer Dean Pomerleau bought a fish instead
of a dog. When his children said fish were boring,
he decided to train Comet. Pomerleau used a wand
with food at the end. For an hour a day, he trained
Comet. After two months Comet was a stunt fish!

21

Tame Tricks by Wild Animals

Unbelievable Pachyderms

Three-year-old elephants in the Maetaeng Elephant Camp and Clinic in Chiang Mai, Thailand, may learn a special stunt: painting! An elephant named Suda paints a self-portrait. She also paints her name. Other elephants named Bank and Srinon paint trees or birds.

Trainers use food, usually bananas, to reward elephants for doing something right. Sometimes, the *mahout* has to demonstrate the stunt. Then the elephant copies the mahout. Some of these intelligent elephants have learned to paint in as little as a month's time.

CHECK THIS OUT! Female Asian elephants stand about 8.5 feet (2.6 m) tall. Males may weigh up to roughly 11,000 pounds (5,000 kilograms). Even at this great size, elephants can walk quietly.

mahout—a person who works with, rides, and tends to elephants

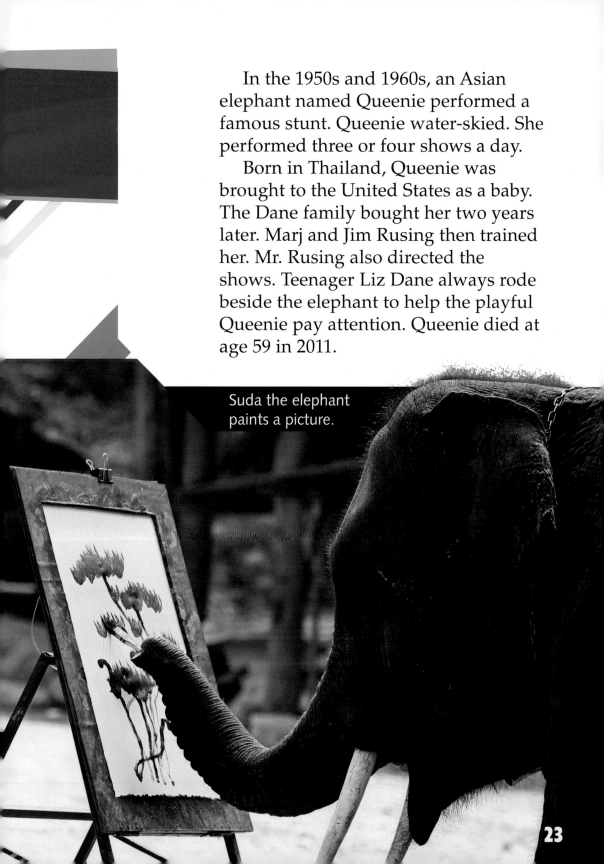

In the 1950s and 1960s, an Asian elephant named Queenie performed a famous stunt. Queenie water-skied. She performed three or four shows a day.

Born in Thailand, Queenie was brought to the United States as a baby. The Dane family bought her two years later. Marj and Jim Rusing then trained her. Mr. Rusing also directed the shows. Teenager Liz Dane always rode beside the elephant to help the playful Queenie pay attention. Queenie died at age 59 in 2011.

Suda the elephant paints a picture.

Monkey See, Monkey Do

Dogs are some of the well-known trained animals. But a company in Massachusetts trains capuchin monkeys for all kinds of stunts. Monkeys' **opposable thumbs** and motor skills give them a big advantage over other animals. Trainers use a laser pointer and words. They reward the monkeys with praise, treats, and *TLC*.

Monkeys are ready for stunts after three to five years of training. They open food containers. They turn pages of a book and open doors. They even know—unlike some humans—how to use technology such as DVD players and computers.

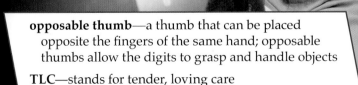

opposable thumb—a thumb that can be placed opposite the fingers of the same hand; opposable thumbs allow the digits to grasp and handle objects

TLC—stands for tender, loving care

What Has Four Legs, Four Wheels, and Squeaks?

Trainer Shane Willmott has trained mice for about 30 years. He started with surfboarding. Now the mice skateboard. Mice are good at both because of their low centers of *gravity*.

Willmott's homemade skating park has ramps and half-pipes. He's even trained his mice to jump through hoops of fire.

gravity—a force that pulls objects with mass together; gravity pulls objects down toward the center of earth

See You In the Movies

Charlie Sammut and his lion, Kaleb, were hired for a part in *George of the Jungle*. Sammut decided to use the "knock-down" training technique for an action scene. The big cat actually knocked down the trainer. The two prepared for several weeks. Kaleb would knock Sammut down. Sammut would stay under Kaleb as long as possible. When it was time to shoot the scene, Kaleb knocked Sammut down. The director then yelled for Sammut to roll the lion onto his back. Sammut obeyed. All went well, and the scene was used in the movie.

Sammut and Kaleb were hired for a different part in *The Postman*. They practiced the knock-down technique at home two times a day. One day when Sammut went down, Kaleb growled. He wouldn't let Sammut off the ground. A tractor finally scared off Kaleb. Sammut suffered a fractured rib, cuts, and bruising.

When it was time to shoot the scene, Kaleb pounced and growled again. Another trainer scared the lion away. Sammut again suffered broken ribs. He decided that the Kaleb's knock-down stunt would have to be retired.

"Many [trainers] choose not to risk doing attack behaviors as it can ruin a cat in the long run, making it aggressive towards all. Instinct can begin to overwhelm training and take over."
Charlie Sammut

Send in the Clowns...and Animals

Lions riding on the backs of horses? Leopards jumping through hoops of fire held in tigers' teeth? Elephants strolling through big-city traffic? These stunts and many more were the handiwork of Gunther Gebel-Williams. This famous animal trainer worked for both The Ringling Brothers and Barnum & Bailey circuses from 1968 to 1990. In this time, he performed about 12,000 shows. He never missed one because he was sick or hurt.

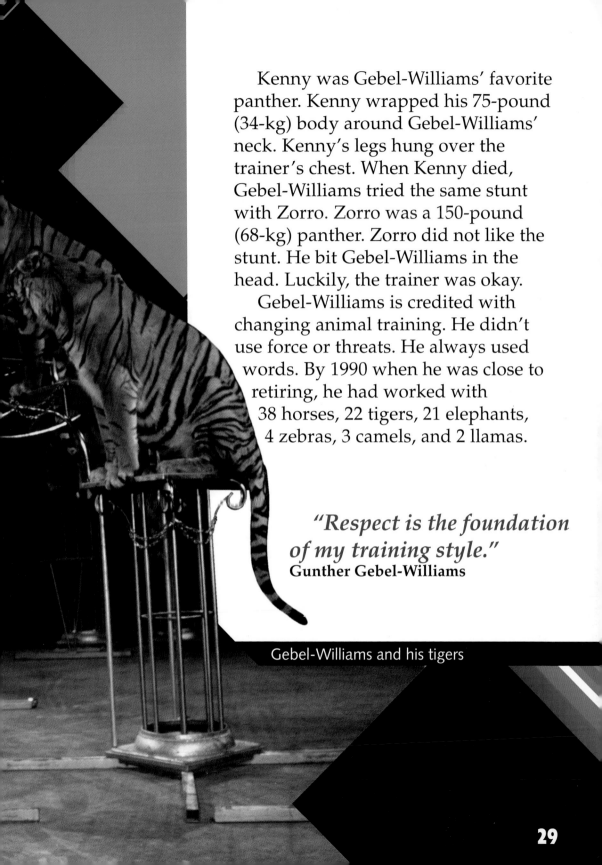

Kenny was Gebel-Williams' favorite panther. Kenny wrapped his 75-pound (34-kg) body around Gebel-Williams' neck. Kenny's legs hung over the trainer's chest. When Kenny died, Gebel-Williams tried the same stunt with Zorro. Zorro was a 150-pound (68-kg) panther. Zorro did not like the stunt. He bit Gebel-Williams in the head. Luckily, the trainer was okay.

Gebel-Williams is credited with changing animal training. He didn't use force or threats. He always used words. By 1990 when he was close to retiring, he had worked with 38 horses, 22 tigers, 21 elephants, 4 zebras, 3 camels, and 2 llamas.

"Respect is the foundation of my training style."
Gunther Gebel-Williams

Gebel-Williams and his tigers

Glossary

canine (KAY-nyn)—of or relating to dogs

chariot (CHAYR-ee-uht)—a light, two-wheeled cart pulled by horses

double dutch (DUH-buhl DUHCH)—a jump-rope game with two long jump ropes swung in opposite directions so that they cross rhythmically

feat (FEET)—an achievement that shows great courage, strength, or skill

feline (FEE-line)—to do with cats

gravity (GRAV-uh-tee)—a force that pulls objects with mass together; gravity pulls objects down toward the center of earth

kneeboard (NEE-bord)—a short board for surfing or waterskiing in a kneeling position

mahout (muh-HOUT)—a person who works with, rides, and tends to elephants

opposable thumb (uh-POZE-uh-buhl THUHM)—a thumb that can be placed opposite the fingers of the same hand; opposable thumbs allow the digits to grasp and handle objects

parachute (PAIR-uh-shoot)—a large piece of strong, lightweight fabric; parachutes allow people to jump from high places and float slowly and safely to the ground

sanctuary (SANGK-choo-er-ee)—a natural area where birds or animals are protected from hunters

stadium jumping (STAY-dee-uhm JUHMP-ing)—a competition where horses and riders follow a course of hurdles or jumps within an arena or riding ring

technology (tek-NOL-uh-jee)—the use of science to do practical things, such as designing complex machines

TLC (TEE EL SEE)—stands for tender, loving care

winged suit (WINGD soot)—a garment that allows a person to glide through the air when in free fall, with sections of fabric between the arms and legs that inflate when the wearer jumps from an aircraft or high place

Read More

125 True Stories of Amazing Pets: Inspiring Tales of Animal Friendship and Four-Legged Heroes, Plus Crazy Animal Antics. National Geographic Kids. Washington, D.C.: National Geographic Society, 2014.

Newman, Aline Alexander. *Animal Superstars: And More True Stories of Amazing Animal Talents.* National Geographic Kids. Washington, D.C.: National Geographic Society, 2013.

Peters, Gregory N. *Real Animal Heroes.* Real World Adventures. North Mankato, Minn.: Capstone Press, 2014.

Townsend, John. *Amazing Animal Communicators.* Animal Superpowers. Chicago: Raintree, 2013.

Internet Sites

FactHound offers a safe, fun way to find Internet sites related to this book. All of the sites on FactHound have been researched by our staff.

Here's all you do:

Visit *www.facthound.com*

Type in this code: 9781491442531

Check out projects, games and lots more at
www.capstonekids.com

Index

animals

    birds, 18, 19, 20

    cats, 5, 14, 15, 26

    chickens, 15, 20

    dogs, 5, 6, 7, 8, 9, 10, 11, 12, 13, 21, 24

    elephants, 5, 22, 23, 28, 29

    goldfish, 21

    horses, 16, 17, 28, 29

    lions, 26, 28

    mice, 25

    monkeys, 5, 24

    ostriches, 20

    owls, 5, 18

    panthers, 29

BASE jumps, 11

Boger, Steve, 20

Carvalho, Clint, 19

circuses, 6, 14, 28

Dane, Liz, 23

Forsythe, Mike, 10

Gebel-Williams, Gunther, 28, 29

Howells, Lyssa, 8, 9

Martin, Samantha, 14, 15

Morales, Captain Alberto, 16, 17, 22

Morgan, Jenny, 18

musical instruments, 5, 14, 15

Pomerleau, Dean, 21

Rusing, Jim, 23

Rusing, Marj, 23

Sammut, Charlie, 26

sports, 13, 20, 21, 25

therapy animals, 17

Uchida, Yoshihiro, 6, 7,

von Muller, Omar, 12, 13

Willmott, Shane, 25